Ordnance Survey Map 1870.

Bygone
ALTON

William Curtis (1803-1881). President of the Mechanics' Institute from its inception in 1837 until his death. Founder of the Curtis Museum in 1855.

Bygone
ALTON

Tony Cross
and
Georgia Smith

Phillimore

1995

Published by
PHILLIMORE & CO. LTD.
Shopwyke Manor Barn, Chichester, West Sussex

ISBN 0 85033 947 2

Printed and bound in Great Britain by
BIDDLES LTD.
Guildford, Surrey

List of Illustrations

Frontispiece: William Curtis (1803-1881)

Acknowledgements

In the compilation of this book we would like to thank the staff of the Curtis Museum and Allen Gallery, Alastair Penfold, Keeper of Hampshire History at the Hampshire County Council Museums Service, for his support and the staff of the Hampshire Record Office who have helped and encouraged us in our research.

Special thanks are due to other colleagues at the Hampshire County Council Museums Service, particularly Trevor Evans, who with skill and good humour has copied and printed much of the photographic material. Wendy Bowen's efforts in maintaining the photographic collection in good order made print selection far easier than it might otherwise have been, and Phyl Brown's keyboard skills and patience ensured the production of the manuscript.

Chris Mardell's permission to use the archives of *Alton Gazette* is gratefully acknowledged.

All of the photographs are in the Hampshire County Council Museums Service collection and sincere thanks are due to all those local people who, over the years, have given photographs or kindly allowed us to copy prints in their possession for the collection.

Introduction

Alton is unique amongst Hampshire's market towns in having a comprehensive photographic record of its development from the mid-Victorian period onwards. Many individual houses and buildings were also recorded and the Curtis Museum has fascinating albums in the collection featuring two local farms.

Photographs used in conjunction with written information can tell us a great deal about our recent past and the people associated with it. Modes of transport, dress, fashion, styles of architecture, shopping habits and much more are recreated through the photographer's lens.

Foremost amongst these was George Frost who opened a photographic studio in Market Street in 1887. When he retired in October 1903 his business was taken over by W.P. Varney who produced a large number of photographic postcards of the town and surrounding area. In January 1910 he, in turn, was succeeded by Mr. H.A. Aylward who maintained the production of postcards of local interest.

Most of those images included here belong to a period long gone and may not have been published before. Inevitably, a few of the photographs have been seen elsewhere but we felt they should be included in the interests of completeness.

A Brief History of Alton

The town of Alton lies in the north east of Hampshire and appears to owe its existence to the source of the River Wey which rises on the edge of the town. The displays at the Curtis Museum include archaeological material from the Stone Age, indicating the local presence of prehistoric hunters. However, it is not until early in Roman times that evidence exists for local settlement.

For nearly four centuries Britain was an outpost of the greatest empire of the ancient world. The impact of Rome was both immediate and long lasting but, locally, only the detailed survey and excavations of the last few years have revealed the full extent of the influence.

A Roman road from Chichester to Silchester ran through the area and a posting station, or *mansio*, was established on the edge of the present village of Holybourne. With the construction of a road from London to Winchester the mansio found itself at the crossroads and, as a consequence, continued to develop. It is thought that it was called *Vindomis*, a name preserved in one of the new developments in Holybourne built over the excavated part of the site.

The main purpose of the settlement was to act as a market centre for the surrounding area but some of the archaeological finds show that longer distance trade routes developed, too. Coin evidence suggests that the town continued in occupation until the 5th century A.D. but was eventually abandoned. The reason for the decline is unknown but the Saxons lived there, too, and their name 'Neatham' is Saxon for cattle market.

A settlement elsewhere in the immediate area of Alton is also a probability due to the discovery of a large Saxon cemetery of seventh-century date at Mount Pleasant in 1959. A selection of the grave goods from this site is on display in the Curtis Museum and includes the Alton Buckle—the finest piece of Anglo-Saxon craftsmanship to have been found in Hampshire.

At the time of the Domesday Survey in 1086, following the Norman Conquest, Alton was a small agricultural community with the advantage of a corn mill on the river. In the course of the next 200 years, the activity along the road between the two capitals of Winchester and London encouraged settlement and changed the cluster of farmsteads into a recognisable town, a status acknowledged by the Royal Command of 1295 to send two burgesses to Parliament.

The Winchester to London road followed the natural line, or outcrop, of gravel which runs from Chawton through to beyond Holybourne. During these early years the streets took shape, barely to alter course down the centuries, and the essential features of medieval life set the pattern of the town and determined its development.

The church of St Lawrence was built in a commanding position on the east side of the river and Alton Eastbrook could have become the nucleus of the town. In 1086 the local market was still at Neatham, now part of Holybourne, but with the growth of population in Alton a site was found for it on the Lord's waste behind the High Street houses in Alton Westbrook. This Saturday market flourished and by 1288, in addition to the stalls, the bailiff himself had a house in the Market Place. The site was more extensive than the modern Market Square and included the area we now know as Market Street. Loe's Alley and Cross & Pillory Lane were approaches to the market between the existing house plots in the High Street. At the same time Lenten Street, originally a track from the Saxon farm at Willhall, developed as the approach to the market from Wyards, Thedden and beyond.

Vital to the life of the community was its field system, essential for agriculture and the creation of a surplus to buy other goods. The tracks leading to the common fields were a basic feature in the town plan. Alton Eastbrook's fields, Great and Little Caker and Longborrow were laid out between the river and the Caker Stream and approached by way of Turk Street. The left fork led along the far bank of the river to Spittal Mill, while the right fork climbed over the hill and then ran down between the strips before dividing again to cross the stream for Worldham, Hartley and Selborne. In time, the fields were extended westwards into Hogpathfield and Borovere, which were served by their own tracks from the main street. The lane to Hogpathfield, now Mount Pleasant, formed the limit of the town's settlement until the 19th century. In Alton Eastbrook the lane to Great Nether Street field, formerly Orchard Lane, acted as a similar limitation to settlement at the other end of the main street.

Today only one medieval route has lost its significance, the lane along the east bank of the river to Tanhouse Lane and through the fields to Shalden. The enclosure of Amery Farm probably curtailed its use and the diversion of the Odiham Turnpike in the early 19th century truncated it.

Records have survived from the beginning of the 14th century relating to houses in the High Street, Turk Street, Lenten Street and the Market Place. Most of them would have been timber-framed buildings with wattle and daub infilling, but one was different and known significantly as Stonehouse. It was on the site of Phillip's Homestore in the High Street, and the shop next door. Wall paintings from an adjacent house have survived and are now exhibited in the Curtis Museum. At about the same time William Trenchaunt, who had come from Normandy, obtained a grant of land next to the river where Currys now stands. A generation later the *Swan Inn* is recorded by name, though it did not extend to a double frontage until the 17th century.

Other tenements were Monk Place and Bulbeck's, almost opposite Stonehouse. These plots in the High Street were relatively large but others in Turk Street and Lenten Street are described as cottages, sometimes with a barn and a few acres in the common fields. A third category, particularly in the market area, were just sufficient in width for a shop front. Living quarters consisted of an open hall behind the shop with perhaps an upper chamber over the shop. As more working or living space was required it was added at the back.

The building on the corner of the Market Square and Cross & Pillory Lane, in early records known as Coppid Hall, contains a timber-framed structure which is probably the only surviving building of the medieval Market Place.

By the end of the 14th century there were some sixteen shops and a number of stalls in or near the Market Place. This activity, combined with that of the merchants living in the High Street and surrounding areas, assured the position of Alton as a market town. Supplies of wool for the cloth trade were available from flocks grazing the surrounding downland.

The trade must have been stimulated by the Italian merchants who were making increasing use of the port of Southampton. Their carts and packhorses passed through the town on their way to London. With them travelled Alton's own merchants bringing in supplies for the dyers and fullers as well as food and wine both to sell and for their own households. By the time the Southampton trade had declined at the end of the 15th century the Alton cloth industry was firmly established and the town could withstand change.

The pattern of early building in the town caused newcomers to be confined within narrow frontages on the High Street and a long line of workshops and stores at the rear which inevitably required access by a back lane.

Nevertheless, a few were able to consolidate quite large holdings close to the centre of the town. Towards the end of the 17th century Benjamin Neave, a wealthy clothier, rented all the buildings from the corner of Market Street down Amery Street to the river. Moses Neave, another clothier in Cross & Pillory Lane, held a five-acre croft behind his house, while William Albery had a farm which is today the site of Westbrook House, the car park and public gardens.

When civil war broke out in 1642, Hampshire, like many other parts of England, had no hard and fast divisions of classes or districts supporting King or Parliament. Large towns were often radical as was the case with Portsmouth and Southampton, whose loss certainly harmed the King's cause. Winchester, with its ancient Royal connections, was loyal to the King. The Marquis of Winchester, John Paulet, maintained the greatest stronghold in the county at his home, Basing House, near Basingstoke.

Under Sir William Waller the Parliamentarians tried to advance to the west early in 1643 and the advance party had reached Winchester and Alton when they heard that a strong Royalist force had set out from Guildford. The Winchester party fell back safely, but a weary Parliamentary force of 200 reached Alton on 22 February, after reconnoitring ahead, when 1,500 Royalist cavalry arrived. The small Parliamentary force sought to surrender but this was refused so they prepared to defend themselves and to inflict as much damage as possible on their attackers. The Parliamentary force was fortunate in having a light cannon which was loaded with musket balls. When the Royalist cavalry advanced the cannon was fired, killing or injuring about eighty, while the others fell back. Although it was getting dark, they attacked again and once more the cannon was fired with devastating effect. It was then too dark for further action and, although the Cavaliers intended to capture the Parliamentary soldiers next morning, the latter escaped silently into the night and rejoined the main army.

Towards the end of 1643 Lord Crawford came to Alton with a regiment of troops to fortify the town for the King, thus protecting Winchester. The troops were under the command of Colonel Bolle and may have been 1,300 strong. Sir William Waller, based at Farnham, decided to attack Alton and by means of a night march surprised the Royalists. Waller had 5,000 cavalry and a regiment of infantry which was reinforced during the day. On 13 December Lord Crawford managed to escape, pursued by the Parliamentary forces. Bitter fighting ensued with the Royalists falling back to the churchyard where they had a defensive position. After some two hours of fierce fighting, the Parliamentary forces managed to enter the church itself where Colonel Bolle was killed along with some of his men. By preventing the formation of a Royalist stronghold at Alton, Parliament was free to use its forces for other purposes, particularly the siege at Basing House, while in Alton the churchwardens were paying for several years to have their building put in order.

Probably the most noticeable change in the appearance of the town took place in the 18th century with the gradual disappearance of the old timber-framed and gabled houses, often with thatched roofs, in favour of brick façades and tiled roofs. Fires were an ever present hazard, particularly in the vicinity of malt houses associated with the brewing trade and the dye houses of the textile industries, and these fashionable improvements were a help in reducing the risks of serious fires.

By the beginning of the 19th century the traditional industry of the town, cloth production, was already in decline, unable to compete with the mills in the north using water power. Before the end of the century another industry, brewing, had come to the fore to make the name of Alton famous.

In 1676 in the parish of Alton there were just over a thousand people over the age of twelve. By 1801 the total population had doubled to just over 2,000 and by 1902 it had more than doubled again to nearly 5,500. Comparison of the 1666 map with the Tithe Commissioners map of 1842 shows that between those years the growth of the town was almost entirely by infilling and the division of existing properties within the established area of the town. Expansion into the fields surrounding the town was prevented by the three types of land holding. The strip system survived in the common fields of Alton long after it had disappeared from the villages, probably because it was well suited to profitable hop growing. In addition, business men in the town still retained many of the earlier enclosures and continued in farming, much of it again hop growing. Furthermore, the boundaries of the large farms were tight upon the existing settlement.

Fortunately, the town was spared the intense pressures of some of the industrial towns held in the unbreakable grip of a powerful landowner. It was the enclosure along the Butts Road which became the site for new building in response to the demand for public services—the Gas Works in 1844 and the police station in 1845. Houses soon followed but expansion was contained within a new boundary, in the 1860s, by the building of the Alton-Winchester railway line. The consolidation of the west end of the town on the other side of Butts Road continued on three separately owned fields occupying the area between the boundary of Willhall Farm and Westbrook House, now Ackender Road and Westbrook Road.

At the east end of the town the old Nether Street field survived, despite the pressure for housing in that area and some of the land continued undeveloped for subsequent generations to use.

One hundred and thirty years ago Alton was a comparatively prosperous, small market town. In 1841 the population was 3,139, ten years later it had risen to 3,528 and, by 1871, 4,092 people lived in the town.

Trade directories of that period reveal a wide variety of shops, crafts, trades and professions which gives the impression of a self-sufficient community. The coming of the railway changed all that and linked the country with the towns, creating a different kind of economy accompanied by far reaching social changes.

One particularly sad mid-Victorian event should be mentioned. Almost everyone has heard of the expression 'Sweet Fanny Adams', meaning 'sweet nothing', but few are aware of its local origin.

The murder in August 1867 of Fanny Adams, an eight-year-old girl who lived in Tanhouse Lane, shocked everyone both locally and nationally. The murderer, Frederick Baker, a young solicitors' clerk, dismembered the child's body and scattered the remains around a hop garden.

When the child failed to return home, a search was organised and the gruesome evidence found. Baker was arrested the same day and eventually brought to trial at Winchester Assizes where he was found guilty and later hanged in front of a crowd of 5,000 people on Christmas Eve 1867. Fanny Adams' headstone, erected by public subscription in 1874, and renovated a few years ago, still stands in the town cemetery on the Old Odiham Road. It might have been our only reminder of the tragic affair had it not been for the macabre humour of British sailors. Served with tins of mutton as the latest shipboard convenience food in 1869, they gloomily declared that their butchered contents must surely be 'Sweet Fanny Adams'. Gradually accepted throughout the armed services as a euphemism for 'sweet nothing' it passed into common usage.

The sale of land at the end of Normandy Street and Anstey Road took place after the building of the school there in 1866. Part of the Victoria Road—Littlefield Road area was laid out for housing but that part of the town did not take shape until after the First World War with the sale of Chauntsingers for council housing.

The expansion of the town may be seen from maps and as it grew various services were introduced. The Sewage works was built in 1861, the Waterworks on Windmill Hill was started in 1876 and gas lighting arrived in 1881.

Communications were improved when telegraphed messages were introduced in 1870. A new post office was built on Crown Hill in 1901 and the town was connected to the National Telephone Network in 1908. Another major innovation was the introduction of electricity in October 1927.

The gradual growth in the size of the town received a boost with the Local Development Plan launched in the mid-1960s. Private building began in the Greenfields and Wootey areas and on Windmill Hill whilst local authority building continued in the area formerly part of Anstey Manor. The construction of the Harp Brewery in the early 1960s was offset by the later decision to cease brewing in the old established breweries. This was a major blow to the town but Alton Urban District Council began to develop the industrial estate in an effort to provide new jobs.

Great swathes of the High Street were demolished and replaced by new buildings which, with hindsight, are not an asset to the town. A new post office and shops were the outcome but the losses included several fine buildings in the High Street including the Manor House, and Lady Place in the corner of the Market Square.

The building of St Mary's church, the opening of the long awaited swimming pool, the new Eggar's Grammar School and the start of work on the bypass, with the finds of Roman pottery, all date from a decade that, perhaps more than any other, changed the face of the town.

However, the historical background still plays a part in the town's development. On the tithe map field 581 is a large enclosure from the common field adjoining the windmill with a dell in one corner—a rare attractive site, close to the town but unspoilt by buildings. It was bought by Frederick Crowley for a new mansion which was completed in 1872 and named Ashdell. In turn, the house became known as Moreland Hall and the Henry Gauvain Hospital. By the 1960s the wheel had turned full circle, for once more Ashdell was a rare attractive site close to the town, a buffer zone to the brewery complex. Now it is part of Alton's new housing. The large farms of Amery, Anstey Manor and much of Willhall have gone for building and the last area available for development was the site of the old common fields of Hogpathfield and Borovere.

At a time when considerable changes have taken place which radically altered the appearance of the town centre, it is interesting to observe changes from an earlier period. The images here show a town that has evolved and developed in an attempt to maintain a position of importance for the benefit of the local community. Long may it continue to evolve and prosper, but at the same time, to have due respect for its past and the heritage of its buildings.

1 Willhall Farm, pictured here in 1898, is one of the oldest documented residential sites in Alton, recorded in Domesday Book in 1086. It had been a Saxon freehold with its own church and a meadow alongside the river. In 1492 it was, amongst other property, bought by Winchester College. The present Georgian house was built of brick made on the site for the Gunner family who farmed there in the 18th and 19th centuries.

2 Another house with origins recorded in Domesday Book was Chauntsingers (originally Cantshangre) of which the last parts were demolished in 1937. Of a timber-frame construction, it stood on a large site in Church Street, now a car park. In front of the house there had been a large barn opening on to the street and around it other farm buildings. Until his death in 1657 Thomas Geale held the lease of Chauntsingers and in 1653 he founded the almshouses on an adjoining site.

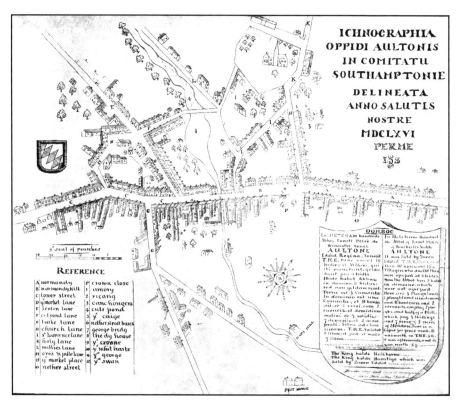

3 This map of 1666 shows all the houses and certain other buildings in the town. It was drawn for the Knight family of Chawton House who held the manors of Alton East-brook and Truncheants. Documentary evidence suggests that, except perhaps for the north side of Market Street, the map is accurate.

4 Amery House was largely an 18th-century building and the former farm of the manor of Alton Eastbrook, although the site may well have been in occupation since the Domesday Survey. The manor belonged to Hyde Abbey, but few records relating to their property in Alton seem to have survived. In 1538, a year before the dissolution, the Abbot granted a 30-year lease to John Hockley, who died three years later. The inventory of his goods provides a description of the house at that time. This engraving dates from 1846.

5 Amery House came into the hands of the Butler family in 1586 and they retained it until 1788, when the house, Amery Farm and 500 acres were sold to Richard Baker for £7,680. The estate was sold again in 1835, and 1888, and eventually the land was sold for housing after the Second World War. The house was turned into flats and it is seen here in 1966. It was demolished in October 1975 and an archaeological excavation was carried out nine years later. After a number of unsuccessful planning applications development eventually took place and the first houses were occupied in 1989.

6 Amery Farmhouse was built in the mid-18th century on the far side of the farm buildings to the west of Amery House. At the time of this photograph, in 1900, it was being farmed by the Chalcraft family. It later became a private residence and the small adjacent area was developed for housing which received the Alton Society John Ambrose Award in 1985. The 18th-century barn in the background was converted into three dwellings linked to two cottages and given the Alton Society Award again, three years later.

7 (*left*) Church Street retains the largest remaining examples of the herringbone-pattern footpath paving laid in the town in 1867, exactly 100 years before this picture was taken. Blue Staffordshire bricks were used, although they were made in Bishops Waltham. On the right lies the old vicarage dating from the early 18th century. It was demolished in October 1967; the present vicarage, built the same year, is on the left.

8 (*right*) St Lawrence's Church dates from *c.*1070, although it has been greatly altered and a spire was added in the 15th century. No trace remains of the medieval cottages on the left which had been demolished by 1830 and the land taken into the kitchen garden of Amery House. In 1973 the new parish hall opened on the site replacing the old corrugated-iron building put up in 1900 in Normandy Street.

9 (*above*) In 1867-8 the church underwent a major restoration at a cost of £3,533, paid for by public subscription. The old 18th-century galleries were removed, the box pews replaced and numerous gifts received including a new organ. Five years later the spire was restored and the lead replaced by oak shingles. The churchyard wall, seen here in April 1868, survived until 1964 when Church Street was widened by 3.5 metres and a new wall and footpath were built.

10 (*right*) Opposite the church were eight cottages, seen here *c.*1890. Subject to leases from 1692, they were sold in 1891 following the death of Thomas Lillywhite. Purchased by Henry Hall, patriarch of the local brewing family, he gave them to his daughter Ethel.

11 (*above*) By the time of the new Ordnance Survey map in 1897 the site, pictured here *c*.1905, had been redeveloped. The iron railings erected in 1883 were victims of the salvage campaigns of the Second World War. The arched ironwork over the gates was made by John (Nimrod) Lock at the beginning of the 19th century. New gates were fitted 40 years ago and they were refurbished in 1986 when new gate posts were needed. The churchyard was levelled in 1957 and 95 stones removed, some to the perimeter wall on the south side. Some of these were repositioned in January 1995.

12 (*right*) This picture of Church Street in 1857 could be the earliest photograph of Alton. On the left is the wall of the *Crown Hotel*, a corner of Dr. Curtis's stable and the garden wall of the old vicarage. On the right are Thomas Geale's almshouses and a row of cottages, since demolished.

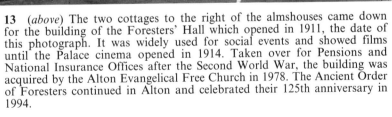

13 (*above*) The two cottages to the right of the almshouses came down for the building of the Foresters' Hall which opened in 1911, the date of this photograph. It was widely used for social events and showed films until the Palace cinema opened in 1914. Taken over for Pensions and National Insurance Offices after the Second World War, the building was acquired by the Alton Evangelical Free Church in 1978. The Ancient Order of Foresters continued in Alton and celebrated their 125th anniversary in 1994.

14 (*left*) It is difficult to recognise this view of *c*.1935 as only the partially hidden building on the left with the distinctive roof remains. The wall of the former Kingdon's yard on the right has been rebuilt, whilst on the left of Baker's Alley there is now a chain link fence. The cottages in the centre were demolished in 1963 as part of the Vicarage Hill road widening scheme.

15 (*below*) This picture of July 1935 is also difficult to place for only the building in the centre remains. A document of 1749 mentions a malthouse consisting of four tenements, a malthouse, courtyard and hog stye adjoining Vicarage Hill. It was given to the Churchwardens for use by the poor of Alton. In 1793, with the opening of the new workhouse at Anstey, they were turned into a hop kiln and stores before becoming part of the site later occupied by Kingdon's. This, in turn, was redeveloped in 1994-5 following the closure of the well known hardware shop some eight years previously.

16 Founded in 1641 by John Eggar of Crondall, the Eggar's School opened the following year. Seen here *c.*1920, it was extended a number of times to increase space, admitted girls in 1911 and became a maintained grammar school within the Hampshire County Council. In November 1968 the school moved into new buildings on the edge of Holybourne, becoming fully comprehensive in 1979.

17 In 1792, land on Anstey Road was bought for £110 and a new workhouse was built at a cost of £4,000. A local Board of Guardians administered the building, seen here *c.*1905, until it and the adjacent Infirmary, built in 1926, were taken over by local government in 1929. The site was used by the Canadian Army in the Second World War and became part of the National Health Service in 1948. Latterly used as accommodation for nurses and as the kitchen for the hospital, the building was sold, renovated in 1985 and converted into sheltered housing.

18 This photograph of *c*.1910 features a column of soldiers, preceded by pipes and drums, marching along Normandy Street. It was published as a postcard by Holliday & Co., photographers of Station Road, and shows the *Barley Mow* before the present wall-hung tiles were fitted.

19 This postcard of *c*.1905 shows what was the edge of the town until the railway arrived in the middle of the 19th century. The *Star Inn*, formerly a Hall's pub, closed in 1907. Two doors along is a printing works, a business carried on in the same premises today. The tree in the centre was outside the Congregational church which was built in 1835 replacing a 17th-century house. The church closed in October 1994 and the site is currently awaiting redevelopment.

20 John Tokely came to Alton about 1880 and ran a pork butcher's a couple of doors up the street. The shop, pictured here *c.*1890, together with the *Star Inn* next door, was eventually demolished to make way for Enticknap's garage, now the premises of a tyre retailer.

21 Lock's Alley, seen here in 1937, formerly ran down the side of the old Congregational chapel and took its name from the family who, for six generations, worked as blacksmiths. In one of these cottages was a huge open fireplace with a decorated beam *c.*1500 across the front. When the cottages were demolished the beam was acquired by the owner of the *Alton House Hotel* and incorporated into a new fireplace in a function room.

22 These mainly 19th-century buildings, photographed in 1959, were demolished to make way for the construction of the new police station and magistrates court which began in 1976.

23 Nether Street, the one-way street seen here, survives today as the footpath down the side of the police station. In this 1959 view is the pub, which closed in January 1966. It used to be called the *Queen Victoria*, but was known as 'the Vic'. In 1867 its name was changed to the *Queen's Arms*.

24 Some of the cottages in Nether Street were pulled down in 1935 as unfit for habitation. At the bottom on the left was the *Rising Sun*, a Complin's pub, which closed in 1907. The single-storey white building on the right, seen here in 1959, with the pantiles, was formerly a blacksmith's shop, but later became a Gospel hall. Derelict, it was demolished in 1985 to make way for new buildings. The shop on the corner was Wells, a photographer's in the 1860s, and later Mr. Marlow's butcher's shop. It was auctioned in October 1907 and bought by Mr. Hayden for £700.

25 The *c*.1960 view towards Normandy Street shows little on the left of the street, now the site of a car park. The trees in the centre, at the top of the street, are those along the edge of Victoria Road on the opposite side of Normandy Street.

26 Blake's Cottages, seen here *c*.1935, were amongst 47 properties in the town condemned under the 1930 Housing Act as unfit for habitation. They were demolished in 1937 and replaced by temporary buildings used by the Red Cross and the Blue Triangle, a boys' club. Later demolished, the site was fronted by hoardings for some years before new housing was built in 1980. The house next door was the YWCA, although it is currently split into a dental surgery and a property known as Alderney House.

27 When this photograph was taken *c*.1880, Mr. Bennett, a dairyman, occupied 26 Normandy Street. He had cowsheds and pig styes at the rear of the premises leading to the lane that formerly led to the Council Yard. This building and the one adjacent with the bow windows are part of a shop subject to a compulsory purchase order on appeal early in 1995. The tall house and the two cottages beyond were demolished to make way for the Victoria Road access *c*.1930.

28 The rather distinguished building in this *c*.1860 view was occupied by a leather cutter at the time. To the left was the *Red Lion* and the side gate provided access to a popular skittle ground, later to become the home of the Alton Quoit Club.

29 A view of the left side of the street *c.*1860 runs from what is now "Teddy's" to Alderney House (next to the cinema). The original *Red Lion* is seen and nearby is the site of another public house, the *Winchester Arms*. On the opposite side of the road next to the *Bell* are the old cottages demolished to make way for Normandy Cottage. The front of Normandy House, with its imposing porch, is on the right.

30 This photograph, *c.*1905, provides a wonderful view west of the side of Normandy Street from the *Red Lion* to the *Barley Mow*. On the east, the view is from the garden of Normandy Cottage to the *Queen's Arms*. The cottages adjacent to Normandy Cottage were acquired for a 1960s' road scheme that did not materialise and, having been derelict for many years, were rebuilt in 1983.

31 The distinctive brickwork of the *Red Lion*, photographed here *c*.1905, has since unfortunately been painted over. It changed from a pub to an off-licence in February 1972, although the replica red lion still adorns the doorway. Judging from the previous picture, it appears to have been rebuilt *c*.1865-79.

32 (*below*) Normandy Cottage, on the extreme left, was built in 1869 as almshouses by Marianna Crowley of Normandy House. The small bunches of fruit in artificial Coade stone are used as 'end stops' to the gothic arch of the doorway, a feature found on many houses of this period in the town. This October 1879 view along the left side of the street shows buildings of many periods, ending with scaffolding poles, the building site of the new Mechanics' Institute and museum.

33 Built about 1822 by Abraham Crowley, founder of Crowley's brewery, Normandy House, seen here *c.*1860, had a large square portico entrance and a row of narrow sash windows on the ground floor to maintain the symmetry. In 1903 this building suffered one of the biggest fires seen in the town and it was again damaged by fire in 1992.

34 (*below*) This view of the buildings at the town end of Normandy Street dates from *c.*1935. The shop with the pointed gable was at one time the 'Universal', later the site of the Co-op. Rebuilt, it became the showroom of the Farnham Gas & Electricity Co., later the Gas Board. They left the town in 1993 and it is now occupied by a religious bookshop. The building to its left was formerly two villas later converted into one. It became two small shops in 1938, which are now reunited as a chemist's. The double-fronted shop in the centre is faced with mathematical tiles, wall-hung tiles in the shape of bricks.

35 In the last picture, to the right of the shop with the pointed gable was a three-storey building. At one time the ironmongery of H.E. Cork, it closed in 1908 and became a butcher's, seen here in 1909. Competition from Mugridge's across the street was fierce and the shop was taken over in 1911 by stepbrothers Charlie Stringer and Bert Tredwell. Ted Tredwell, son of one of the founders, carried on the business until he retired in June 1981 and, although it continued to be a butcher's for a short time, it later became the premises of an estate agency.

36 (*above right*) This view *c*.1890 shows what was on the site before the building with the distinctive gable. It was initially occupied by Mr. Bransby, who had a corn and seed shop and a successful grocery shop next door. This was later taken over by George Southern and, interestingly, both names can be seen on the shop.

37 (*below right*) The extended shop front of 8 Normandy Street, seen here *c*.1890, suggests expansion. Later Mr. Southern moved to the other side of the road, and subsequently the business was acquired by John Channin.

38 The increasing interest in the internal combustion engine can be seen in this *c.*1920 view, with a motor-cycle dealer on the corner and, directly opposite, a garage with a sign for BP petrol. However, the parked cars and motorcycles did not yet outnumber the bicycles.

39 This view of a similar scene and date also has bicycles, cars, and two delivery lorries, although the traffic is not exactly heavy. The Westminster Bank and Messrs A.W. Moore are sharing the distinctive Georgian building on the right.

40 (*right*) Channin and Harris had a grocery business at 3 Normandy Street next to the garage, pictured here in August 1941. The house with the bow window seen in earlier views was later two shops which were rebuilt into one around 1900 by Mr. Mugridge, a butcher. A garage remained on this site until 1985 when it became available for development. Although permission for a supermarket was approved in 1990, nothing materialised due to the decision of Sainsbury's to come to Alton. Development eventually took place and the new building was occupied in 1994.

41 (*below*) The earliest records of Rodney House date from 1676 when it was sold by William Simpson to William Wake, in whose family it remained for 90 years. It was acquired in 1766 by James Rodney, brother of Admiral Rodney of Alresford. In this George Frost photograph are Betsey Blake and her family, with the house decorated for Queen Victoria's Diamond Jubilee in 1897.

42 With current volumes of traffic it is difficult to imagine Church Street, seen here *c*.1935, at half of its present width. However, until the mid-1960s there was a row of cottages fronting on to Church Street from the old Foresters' Hall down to the corner.

43 The view down Church Street towards Normandy Street *c*.1960 shows the exact width of the road. Some of the cottages were demolished early in 1962, but it took until the spring of 1966 before the road widening and corner improvement were completed.

44 The *Crown Hotel* has been refronted and the doors repositioned since this was taken *c*.1900, but it is of 15th-century origin and retains inside some of its early timbering.

45 Until the 18th century Crown Close encompassed all of the land from the top of the hill down to the entrance to the present Manor car park, across to Great Nether Street field and the river, an area of about three acres. The building seen in this 1845 drawing was the 'Caige', the town's lock up. Its most frequent use was to hold vagrants overnight before escorting them out of the parish. Standing beside it was a small brick house, probably intended for a part-time jailer.

46 By the 1870s Crown Close belonged to Hall's Brewery. The field pictured here in 1878 had become the site for visiting fairs and circuses and for displays of fireworks whenever there was a celebration. On the far side towards the river the Curtis family had a small farm. Henry Hall had enclosed the rest of the land in the extensive park and gardens of the Manor House. In 1877 there was a pressing need for new public buildings and the land adjoining Crown Hill was donated by Mr. Hall.

47 The buildings on Crown Close—the Mechanics' Institute and museum, the Inwood Cottage Hospital and the Assembly Rooms, were achieved within three years. Designed by Mr. C.E. Barry, the local firm of J.H. and E. Dyer were awarded the building contract and work began in 1879. All three buildings were opened in October 1880, and are seen here in June 1882.

48 On Jubilee Day, Tuesday 21 June 1887, following a thanksgiving service at St Lawrence's Church, crowds gathered outside the public buildings. Three cheers were called for the Queen by Gerald Hall, Chairman of the local Jubilee Committee. There was also a schools' procession followed by sports and a tea.

49 William Curtis and his family are seated in the garden of 4 High Street, now part of the garden at the rear of the Allen Gallery. The founder of the museum is on the extreme left and his eldest son, also William, is second from the right in this 1866 picture. He followed his father into his medical practice and supported the museum. In 1896 he published the *History of Alton*, still required reading for anyone interested in local history.

50 William Curtis (1803-1881), the first President of the Mechanics' Institute in 1838, was the fourth generation of a family of doctors who had practised from the same house in the High Street since 1720. He is seen here setting out on his rounds *c*.1870.

51 The Mechanics' Institute, pictured here *c*.1900, occupied the ground floor of the new building and the museum was on the upper floor in the two large rooms. William Curtis, the founder of the museum, died on 7 October 1881, aged 79, and in his memory it was decided that it should be known as the Curtis Museum.

52 (*above*) The Georgian façades of 4-10 High Street, seen here *c*.1900, hide the evidence of older houses like many of Alton's buildings. The steps from the raised pavement were later removed for safety. Note the white, corner premises at the High Street—Market Street junction and the one with the angled frontage on the left about half way down Crown Hill.

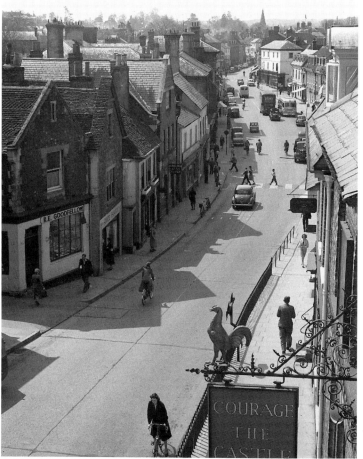

53 (*left*) Superficially little has changed in this *c*.1960 view, but the curve in the road hides many buildings that were replaced in the 1960s. The pub on the right no longer exists and Goodfellows' butcher's shop went to provide access to the new car park behind the Manor House, a few doors along.

54 With muddy streets and cobbled pavements the town could not have been pleasant for pedestrians when this photograph was taken *c.*1860. The carving of the Lion and Unicorn adorns the shop known as King's Library.

55 It is interesting to note the differences in this similar view eight years later. The repaving of the town had an obvious effect and the building next to King's Library now has another storey. This grocer's and butcher's shop was kept by Henry Vandell and was rebuilt in 1901 to become the post office.

56 The post office had a date stone of '1901' high on the gable which is not visible in this 1907 view looking up Crown Hill, although it can still be seen on the building today. The brickwork has since been painted and it has lost its distinctiveness. The buildings on the opposite side of the road include Munday's saddler's shop with the sun blind, at 18 High Street, formerly the *White Hart Hotel*.

57 The edge of the 1928 shop front of the former Kingdon's hardware shop provides the reference point for this *c*.1930 view up Crown Hill. Fishmonger, greengrocer, shoe shop, fruiterer and saddler occupied this range of 18th- and 19th-century buildings until they were demolished in 1967 and replaced by the present buildings. The 'gap-site' on Crown Hill comprises 18 and 20 High Street, the tall white building and the one next door with the two bay windows on the first floor.

58 On the extreme right, the edge of the *Baker's Arms* locates this July 1963 photograph of the demolition of Kerridge's Garage. Then, as now, the river flowed in a culvert under the building and the road. Kerridge's moved into the High Street in 1910 and subsequently developed the site. It was sold in 1962 and they moved to Tews Garage (at one time Fenton's) on Butts Road, where they re-opened in May 1963.

59 The Georgian appearance of this part of the High Street, seen here in 1957, is somewhat deceptive, for many of these buildings have been rebuilt as the dates on the top of their drainpipes indicate. Barclays Bank was formerly Chesterfield's shop, Lloyds Bank was once known as *Conduits Temperance Hotel*, the National Provincial Bank was once owned by Mr. Farthing and the site of the Westminster Bank was at one time a cake and bun shop.

60 Alton celebrated the wedding of the Prince and Princess of Wales on 10 March 1863 with a magnificent triumphal arch across the High Street. The wooden framework was covered in trees and evergreens and the day was a general holiday with celebrations followed by a bonfire and firework display in the evening. The old town pump, which stood directly over the river, can be seen on the right between the gas lamp and the children.

61 There were a number of private banks in Alton before the amalgamations which have given rise to those of the present day. The grouping represented here on 36 High Street *c*.1919 came about in 1918, and the following year they applied for permission to alter the building. It became the Westminster Bank in 1923 and merged with the National Provincial Bank to form National Westminster Bank in 1968.

62 Founded in 1877, Chesterfield's building originally had ordinary sash windows and the shop only occupied the two front rooms. Over the years it expanded and eventually had an adjoining boot department in 44 High Street, seen here in 1907. The rear of this property was skilfully redeveloped in 1985 and won the Alton Society John Ambrose Award.

63 The demolition in March 1967 of 46 High Street, formerly occupied by Downie and Gadban, solicitors, allowed the inclusion of yet another undistinguished building in an important part of the town centre.

64 The imposing façade of the Manor House, is the obvious feature of this *c.*1900 picture, but a closer look at the other buildings reveals a collection of both quality and diversity. Most of them, including the Manor House, have been replaced by an assortment of structures.

65 Built *c*.1842-50 on the site of the *White Hart*, the Manor House seen here *c*.1900, was occupied by the Hall family until April 1926. Major Courage purchased the house and grounds and the house was used by the Co-op from 1931. They demolished the building in 1968 and re-opened a new department store on the site the following year. Changes in retailing saw the closure of the grocery business in 1984 and two years later the store closed completely. The building is currently occupied by Southern Electric and Currys.

66 Documentary evidence shows that the *Swan Inn* existed in 1498, but the house was already 100 years old. An adjacent house was acquired in the 16th century and it became a flourishing coaching inn with access to the yard to the right of the buildings.

67 The purchase of a large house on the other side of their gateway by Roger Harrison and his son Thomas in the late 17th century was a shrewd move. The *Swan* was later acquired by John Hawkins, who rebuilt the original houses to the left of the gateway, leaving untouched the large gabled house on the other side seen in this sketch of 1845.

68 In the early 19th century the big courtyard of the *Swan* was the scene of great activity as stage coaches clattered under the archway from London, Gosport and Southampton bringing passengers, parcels and mail. There were 19 rooms and the inn boasted the biggest stabling accommodation in the town for the coaches and travellers as well as competing for the custom of local people. This view dates from *c.*1890.

69 Henry Hall purchased the Hawkins brewery in 1841 and the *Swan* was largely rebuilt. Much of the large gabled house was pulled down to make way for an enlarged hotel and a newly positioned gateway seen here in 1900. The front door received a portico and to the left an extension was built which faithfully matched the features of Hawkins' inn.

70 Pictured here is the other side of the triumphal arch for the royal wedding between Prince Albert Edward, later King Edward VII, and Princess Alexandra, eldest daughter to the heir of the Danish throne. The three-storey 19th-century brick building on the right was known as Regent House and is a useful reference point in old photographs of the High Street. On the left, note that the premises on the corner with Market Street has two storeys.

71 The view from the Turk Street corner in 1872 gives a good impression of Victorian Alton. Many of the buildings on the right remain today, although they have modern shop fronts. The *Royal Oak* inn sign is attached to the building on the right-hand corner of Turk Street.

72 (*above*) In the 19th century the premises later known as Johnson's corner, seen here in 1959, were formerly occupied by a number of drapers including J.C. Jefferis, Holman, George and Walter Castle and H. Charmain. In the spring of 1977, archaeologists dug inside the shop and evidence of medieval Alton was uncovered. The site was redeveloped and Boots opened a new shop on the corner in 1980.

73 (*right*) It is interesting to compare this *c.*1900 view with that in no. 70 and see the renovations and, in the case of 39 High Street, the complete rebuild from a two-storey tiled cottage to the massive three-storey building currently occupied by Phillip's. Two previous occupants, Charles Ginger and Hewitt & Sons, were also ironmongers. The building on the left, with the blind arch above the door, was known as 'Bulbecks'.

74 (*above*) The original 1930s' Woolworth store photographed here in April 1976 was built on the site of 'Bulbecks'. Porter's now occupy the site of Smead, the wine merchants, who acquired it in 1931 from Mr. Loe. On the other side of Loe's Alley was the Timothy White store, although, when they amalgamated with Boots, Boots moved into this site from 35 High Street and stayed until 1980.

75 The *Royal Oak* on the Turk Street corner was rebuilt in the 19th century and provides a convenient reference point in this picture of *c*.1880. Next door, 55 High Street was probably built *c*.1581 and was originally gabled and jettied. The roof was turned and a new brick façade built, probably in the 18th century. Formerly occupied by Bartlett and Butcher, the site was renovated and in 1989 Stoodley's relocated here from Crown Hill.

76 The light-coloured buildings on the left of this *c.*1865 view were pulled down in 1930-31 and on the site Martin and Stratford built new offices and an entrance to the market. The brick building next door, at 66 High Street, was formerly the post office. On the right the double-fronted house (with the ladder) is called 'Swarthmore'. Its early history is associated with James Baverstock who made his name as a local brewer and probably built the house in 1770.

77 (*left*) Julius Caesar was born in Alton in 1852 and followed his father, William, into the hairdressing business he founded in 1859, acquiring 66 High Street in 1877, possibly the date of this photograph. As a young man he joined the newly established Volunteer Fire Brigade as a messenger and later the bugler. He was also well known as a cricketer following a long family tradition.

78 (*right*) A slightly older Julius Caesar stands proudly in the doorway of his re-designed shop front in 1908. On his death in 1927 his son took over the business and part of the premises remained as a hairdresser's, trading under the same name until 1988 when they were converted to offices. However, the renovated building is called Julius Caesar House.

79 Lansdowne House, on the left of this 1877 street scene, was built *c.*1740 by William Wotey. His father, also William, had owned the *George Inn* (on the site of the present Army and Navy Stores) as well as being a farmer. Some of his former land was built over as part of the Wootey Estate.

80 Between 1890 and 1901 the post office occupied 72 High Street. Next door was Lansdowne House which seems to have been a popular residence for local doctors before becoming the Midland Bank in 1952. Opposite, in this view *c.*1890, are the premises of the Row family who had been clockmakers in various buildings in the town since the end of the 19th century.

81 The ivy-covered building on the left of this *c*.1910 view is Rawdon House, formerly the residence of Edward Dyer, a partner of the well known local building firm. In the centre is Westbrook House, the remodelled medieval farmhouse of the manor of Alton Westbrook and, later, a private lunatic asylum. The buildings on the right have all been demolished and the site has been redeveloped.

82 Westbrook House was acquired by Alton Urban District Council (AUDC) in 1931. They pulled down part of it and widened Cross and Pillory Lane. The AUDC also converted the building into offices, built on the fire station, made an entrance into the grounds and constructed a car park for 100 cars at the rear. The building seen here *c*.1950 remained in local authority control until 1976 and the fire brigade moved out in 1981.

83 There is a rather run down appearance in this *c.*1960 photograph of 70-76 High Street including Rawdon House without its ivy, although the *Alton Mail* did renovate 76 High Street. They previously had offices in Normandy Street and in 1966, when the *Hampshire Herald and Alton Gazette* became simply the *Alton Gazette*, they changed their name to the *Alton Herald*. The site was cleared in advance of the redevelopment of new shops which were built in 1963.

84 Old cottages, seen here in 1935, next to 76 High Street were also demolished at that time. However, the access to Coombes Cottages, formerly behind the High Street, became widened into the present-day roadway alongside the *White Horse* leading to the car park.

85 Nos. 65-67 High Street is seen here in 1966 shortly before demolition. The site, now part of Woolworths, was formerly associated with Keymarkets. No. 63 High Street, on the extreme left, dates from 1763 and is currently a shop and the offices of Bradley Trimmer, solicitor. He was Town Clerk for 40 years, retiring in 1944, and, confusingly, occupied 65 High Street before moving to 61 High Street in 1932. That building was renovated by his successors in 1981 and is now occupied by Porter's. Arthur Hay's radio business began in Market Street in 1934. He later took over Wilson Webb's shop at 65 High Street. Following the re-development, he moved to Turk Street and retired in 1978.

86 News of the relief of Mafeking reached Alton early on Saturday 19 May 1900, three days after the event. Before 9 a.m. the town was ablaze with red, white and blue and the Volunteer Band played in the streets. There were great celebrations and the decorations were left up for the Queen's birthday on the following Thursday. With the exception of the *Hop Poles* pub in the distance, nothing else remains of this scene.

87 The distinctive doorway of 71 High Street could be seen in the previous picture and its location is helped by the position of the post office in this 1966 photograph.

88 The 1965 post office was built on the site of Westfield, the white building on the right of this *c.*1910 picture. It was formerly the home of William Dyer, one of the founders of the building business, and later Mr. Farthing, who had a shop where the Oxfam Shop is currently located. There had been a shop on Lovell's site, 75 High Street, since at least 1666 and it was rebuilt in 1909. The small datestone between the upper windows was revealed when the premises, which nestle between the post office and a supermarket, were redeveloped in 1982.

89 Two doors along was Frenche's Court, a small development running back behind 79 High Street, seen here *c.*1935. At the end was the Philanthropic Hall which could accommodate 60 people, much used for temperance meetings, and later occupied by the Plymouth Brethren before they moved to Vicarage Hill. There was also a cottage used at one time as the HQ of the YWCA.

90 The *White Horse* provides a point of reference for this view of *c.*1911 which has changed considerably. At one time the landlord hired carts and the stabling he used for his horses was at the back of the building. The horses were taken in across the pavement and through the entrance to the public house. As the door was so low, the horses had to be told to lower their heads when they went in.

91 (*above*) Built in 1846 at a cost of £850 the Wesleyan chapel, seen here *c*.1890, provided a permanent place of worship for the group who came to Alton in 1842. The last service was held in March 1976. The building was demolished the following year and a supermarket opened on the site in 1979.

92 (*above*) A new Methodist church was built behind the supermarket and a 'time capsule' was buried in a vintage biscuit tin beneath the foundations in October 1979. In this *c.*1900 view next to the original chapel were the premises of D.J. Kemp & Son, builders, and successors to J.M. Dyer & Sons. Roman pottery was found on the site in 1867 and, when the buildings were demolished in 1980, in connection with the construction of Draymans Way, an excavation uncovered part of a Roman burial ground. Some of the material found is on display in the Curtis Museum.

93 (*left*) The building on the left edge of this *c.*1890 picture in Butts Road was the town's first hospital, opened in 1868, although it later became the home of Mr. Pearce who owned the adjacent sawmill. The shop and post office was occupied by a number of people including Mr. Southern and later R.C. Godfrey, although in more recent years it has had varied uses.

94 Ackender House, partially obscured by the mature trees in this 1947 view, was a boarding school from the middle of the 19th century, but later became the family home of Major Godfrey Burrell MC who died in 1931. Pearce's sawmills were on the opposite corner of Ackender Road and, in time, the site was replaced by two garages. The corner shop and post office was originally a private house and the projecting shop front was added when W. Southern owned the shop.

95 Miss Bell's fountain at the Butts was erected in 1879 opposite the lane to her house at Borovere. The toll house at the Butts had been demolished and with it the only street light. So Miss Bell commissioned a design from Sir Charles Barry for a fountain incorporating a light to stand on a piece of her land. The view behind is of the fields on Whitedown which stretched away to Willhall Farm in this view of *c.*1880.

96 Pictured here in May 1920 is the old road to Winchester which formerly ran along the right side of the Butts, then Chawton Park Road, and through Chawton Park woods. When the turnpike was established in 1753 it was routed along the left of the Butts, Winchester Road and through Chawton. This road was later truncated due to the construction of the bypass which opened in 1971.

97 This postcard view of the Butts, *c.*1900, gives an indication of the almost rural nature of the area. The cottages on the left were built *c.*1880 and originally known as 1-6 The Beeches, after the beech hedge along their roadside boundary.

The Butts, Alton.

98 The Butts, pictured here *c*.1900, consists of about four acres and was acquired from the Hon. John Dutton, Lord of the Manor of Alton Westbrook, on a 99-year lease by the Alton Local Board in 1882. It is thought that the horse chestnut trees were planted around this time. The manorial rights were subsequently given to Alton Town Council in 1981 by Mr. Ralph Dutton, lord of the manor at that time.

99 The brick and thatch cottages opposite the Butts, by the *French Horn*, seen here in April 1935, were probably built in the late 18th century. They do not appear in a report of a perambulation around the parish of Alton in June 1746, for at that time the Chawton boundary lay along the west end of the Butts. The adjacent *French Horn* is first mentioned in a document of 1802 and appears to have been named after a family of the same surname who lived on the site for much of the 18th century.

100 (*above*) 'Of all the crops the farmer has to do with, this is the most interesting, causes him more anxiety, requires more attention, costs more to produce and perhaps oftener fails than any other; but at the same time no crop has paid so well.' Journal of William Terrell Gunner of Willhall Farm, 18 August 1850. Hops have been extensively grown in the Alton area for over 200 years and probably much longer. Now only a few hop gardens remain and seen here is Mr. Andrews laying out hop poles at Willhall Farm in 1903.

101 (*right*) The hop plant was formerly grown up tall poles set on small mounds called hills. This 1903 hop garden may have contained many hundreds of hills with two or three poles to each hill and several hop bines to each pole.

102 Hop picking usually began in the last days of August or early September. As there was insufficient local labour, large numbers of people and even whole families migrated from London, Portsmouth or Southampton for the picking weeks. It was considered by some to be a paid holiday. All Saints' Church can be seen in this 1880 view and Butts Road runs left to right across the middle of the picture.

103 The hops were picked into five or seven bushel baskets then emptied into surplices, seen here in 1880, before being checked by the tallyman. They were then taken to the kiln to be dried. The hops were spread over a hair cloth laid across the upper floor of the kiln. Hot air from the furnace beneath rose through the cloth to dry the hops. Until recently sulphur was added during drying to give the hops an even, yellow colour.

104 Once the hops had cooled they were gently shovelled through a hole in the floor into a long cylindrical sack called a pocket which hung from the ceiling of the room below. The hops were pressed into the pocket by a machine, although formerly this had been done by treading them down. Seen here is a load of hops from Amery Farm in 1901.

105 (*right*) During the last quarter of the 19th century systems of wirework, string and poles gradually replaced the traditional and less productive method of growing. Stilts, or steps, were often used to tie the strings to the tops of the wirework.

106 (*below*) Both of the town's large breweries were situated in Turk Street and the workers of Hall's, the smaller of the two, are seen here *c*.1890. Henry Hall bought the brewery, and the pubs attached to it, from John Hawkins in 1841. The woollen hats worn by some of the men have been 'adopted' by the Alton Morris men.

107 Courage bought Hall's brewery in 1903 when annual production was 20,000 barrels a year. Brewing took place in the buildings behind the cottages in this view looking up Lower Turk Street towards the High Street *c.*1910. With the arrival of the railway it became possible to reach the London markets and later a siding was constructed which served the adjacent breweries. The locomotive working the siding was owned by Courage and is featured on the hanging sign of *The Railway*, formerly a Courage pub.

108 (*below*) Courage gradually developed the brewery and this scene of *c.*1920 is the same view as the previous photograph. The buildings on the left of the road consisted of the maltings, storage premises, the maintenance department and a special loading dock for railway wagons. Until 1973 there was also a stable with six dray horses and a fine collection of harness.

109 Peak production was reached in 1950 when output was 250,000 barrels. However, in 1969 brewing was transferred to Courage's new Reading brewery and Alton became a canning, kegging and distribution depot. Bass Charrington acquired the brewery in 1979, demolished much of it and built a new kegging plant which opened in 1982. A new brewhouse was added nine years later. Seen here *c.*1910 are the Courage & Co. offices at the entrance to the old brewery in Turk Street.

110 The Crowley brewery building, seen here c.1890, was formerly on the site of the tower which was constructed in 1901. It was a difficult operation as the foundations had to be formed in poor ground conditions. Many hundreds of tons of cement were washed away before the solid foundations could be consolidated and eventually the tower had to be supported on a brick arch.

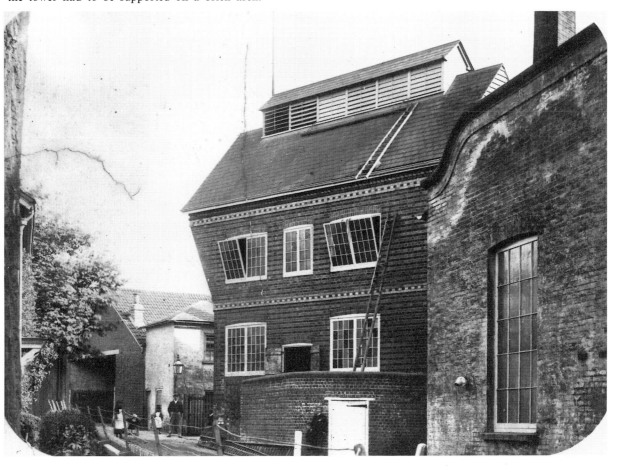

111 In 1763 James Baverstock, with his son, built a brew house in Turk Street. This was bought by Abraham Crowley in 1821 and in 1877 it was acquired by H.P. Burrell who had married into the family. It signalled the start of a period of development and expansion, for between 1878 and 1902 six other local breweries and their public houses were taken over. The brewery is seen here *c*.1910.

112 Workers in the cask washing shed *c*.1910. The brewery was acquired by Watney, Combe, Reid & Co. Ltd. in 1947 and, although production ceased in 1970, it was used as a distribution depot by Watney's and later the renamed Phoenix Brewery Company. The site closed in 1991 and was redeveloped by Sainsbury's who opened their supermarket in 1992.

113 The former chalk pit near King's Pond with its growth of trees, seen here *c.*1864, was the original Ashdell. It was later used as the name for the nearby house and, later still, the road itself. This is the scene before the former was built and the railway extended to Winchester. Note the footpath running up the hill in the middle distance.

114 Following the building of Ashdell, the footpath ran across the grounds in front of the house. Frederick Crowley had it re-routed out of sight around the back and down newly-built steps, the route it still follows today. The bridge, seen here *c.*1905, connected the grounds with King's Pond. It was taken down for safety reasons after the First World War.

115 The view from King's Pond *c.*1900 gives a good indication of the impressive location of Ashdell. Built by J.H. & E. Dyer for Frederick Crowley in 1872, a carriage drive, planted with an avenue of *Wellingtonia*, ran through the centre of the estate which divided the park from the lawns. The trees are still a notable feature today.

116 Frederick Crowley, third of Abraham Crowley's four sons, was born in Normandy House in July 1825 and shared a love of natural history with his cousin, William Curtis, later founder of the museum. He was a President of the Mechanics' Institute and retired from the family brewing business in 1877. The house is pictured here *c.*1890.

117 Following the death of Frederick Crowley in 1910 the house and its grounds, seen here *c*.1890, were acquired by Mr. Guy Ferrand who renamed it Moreland Hall. In 1925 it became a clinic run by Sir Henry Gauvain of the Lord Mayor Treloar Hospital. After his death in 1945 it was renamed the Gauvain Clinic and, later, the Gauvain Hospital. It became surplus to requirements in 1963 and was demolished six years later to make way for a housing development.

118 Three sons of Abraham Crowley of Normandy House married three sisters from the Curtis family along the road at 4 High Street, so there were close links between these two Quaker families. In addition, the Curtis family intermarried with the Chalcrafts, farmers at Amery Farm so it is not surprising that this Crowley family photograph of 1870 was rather crowded.

119 Although it was on the High Street, the main door of the Manor House, seen here *c.*1900, faced into the gardens which stretched all the way to the railway line near King's Pond. Part of the area was fenced off and a small herd of deer were kept. There were also extensive glass houses and a splendid kitchen garden.

120 Mrs. Henry Hall, touring the grounds of the Manor House in a donkey cart *c.*1900, is quite a contrast to the present-day Bass brewery which extends over the former park. The area at the rear of Curry's premises, which were built on the site of the Manor House, is known as the Manor car park—a link with an important piece of local history.

121 The visit to Alton by Princess Louise, Duchess of Argyle, in October 1904 caused quite a stir. After arriving by train, the royal party drove to the Manor House for lunch where they were received by Mr. Goodwyn Hall. Her Royal Highness later opened an exhibition at the Assembly Rooms and, after staying overnight in Froyle, the royal party paid a visit to the Princess Louise Hospital before returning to London by train.

122 Anstey Manor was bought by Henry Hall in 1879. However, the original building was demolished by Gerald Hall after he had acquired it from his father in 1898 and the house, seen here *c.*1910, was built. Following his death in 1940 it was requisitioned for Army use and after the Second World War the house and 69 acres were bought for £12,000 by the AUDC. They kept the land and sold the house to the Convent of Our Lady of Providence for £6,000 and the new school was opened in January 1946.

123 The line of the High Street running left to right and the large, square Manor House provide reference points for the layout of the Courage brewery and its railway siding in this 1952 aerial view. Culverton House on Lower Turk Street lies behind the two long sheds in the right foreground and in the bottom right corner is the road bridge over the railway on Windmill Hill.

124 Viewed from the west, the Courage brewery occupies the centre of this 1952 photograph and part of the Watney's site with the tower lies to the top right. The roof of the *Swan Hotel* can be seen in the bottom right corner and the Windmill Hill railway bridge is visible in the top left.

125 The Watney's brewery tower dominated the skyline until its demolition, although the Courage buildings were of considerable height as this *c.*1972 view from Crown Hill shows. The flat roof of the new Co-op building is evident, as is the new Manor car park behind it. The widened access to the latter from Crown Hill is also seen.

126 In 1861 Thomas Piper of Alresford took over the grocer's and baker's shop of William Grove, housed in an 18th-century building on the corner of High Street and Market Street, seen here in 1886. At that time it was known as Grove's Corner, for William had been trading there since 1824 following his marriage to Kezia Harrow the previous year. Her family had operated a bakery on the site in the early 19th century.

127 These premises were rebuilt before this picture of *c.*1920 was taken, enabling Alfred Piper to have a window in Market Street as well as on the High Street. Following his death, the site was sold in December 1926 and acquired by John Farmer Ltd. The date '1956' on a drainpipe in Market Street denotes the most recent rebuilding on the site, although it is still a shoe shop.

128 The 1977 excavations at Johnson's Corner revealed a complex history of individual buildings since the 16th century. No. 2 Market Street was thought to be 17th-century with a partial rebuild in the 19th century. The former *Plough Inn*, at 4 Market Street had 17th-century origins, although it had a 19th-century façade. The tall building with the sack hoist was Loe's bakery, completed in 1900, although previous buildings seem to have been on the site since the 16th century. Nos. 10, 12 and 14 Market Street had similar origins with later rebuilding obscuring earlier details, a feature of many of the town's 'Victorian' buildings.

129 This George Frost photograph of *c*.1890 shows the outside of his shop at 7 Market Street which he bought in 1878. The directory of that time describes him as a grocer, provision dealer, emigration agent, newspaper correspondent, insurance agent and secretary of the Foresters' Friendly Society.

130 (*above*) F.W. Kerridge bought the established cycle and motor cycle business of S.G. Watkins at 9-11 Market Street in April 1907. The track alongside his shop provided access to the rear of the High Street where he rented stables at the rear of what is now Lloyds Bank. By 1910 he had acquired 36 High Street and opened a cycle shop and garage, and in succeeding years expanded into 34 and 32 High Street, rebuilding them as a car showroom. In time he developed workshops at the rear and access to Vicarage Hill adjacent to Baker's Alley.

131 (*right*) At the present time there is a greetings card shop on the corner of the lane which leads from Market Street to the Banks car park. Before the shop was built *c*.1880, the site was occupied by the woodlapped hop kiln seen here. This, and the adjacent area, was a farm formerly the property of Benjamin Geale, a member of the prominent family of mercers and farmers in the town, who died in 1761.

132 On the left in this 1878 picture of Market Street was the home of the Clinker family of blacksmiths. For a hundred years they had operated a smithy at the rear with access down an alley from the Market Square. A footpath to the smithy ran along the side of their property and it is still a right of way today beside the newsagent's shop. The house beyond the one with the double bay windows was occupied by the Mechanics' Institute and Adlam's bakery was yet to be modernised.

133 (*above*) John Allen seen here at his shop in Market Street *c.*1870, was the grandfather of William Herbert Allen, one time principal of Farnham Art College. When he died in 1943 he left to the Curtis Museum a collection of paintings and his name was given to the Gallery in Church Street where a selection of his work is on view.

134 (*above*) This view of Market Street on 8 May 1920 shows the rebuilt bakery on the corner of the Market Square. After a variety of uses it became a bakery in 1851 when it was acquired by William Dogerall. In 1888 he sold it to Henry Adlam in whose family it remained until acquired by Paul Buck and his father in 1963. They carried on the trade as a bakery until Easter 1991, since when it has had a variety of uses.

135 (*left*) Bertram Caesar, son of Julius, opened a newsagent's shop at 16 Market Street in 1912, two years before this picture was taken. In partnership with his sister they opened another shop at 63 High Street in 1920. The partnership was later dissolved and she ran the original premises, whilst he looked after the High Street site. He was a well known local figure and spent nearly 20 years on AUDC. He retired in 1960 and died six years later at the age of 80.

136 Bought in March 1855 by the Mechanics' Institute, 18-20 Market Street became the site of Alton's first museum, opening its doors to the public on 1 January 1856. When it moved to Crown Close in 1880, the building was sold to James Butler, a grocer. By the time this picture was taken *c*.1900 it was George Gates butcher's shop. It had a long history in this trade until E. Morgan & Son moved to the High Street in January 1995.

137 This 1878 picture of Market Street provides a good view of the street from the Town Hall to the High Street. The buildings are of varied date with 19th-century brick façades hiding earlier timber-framed structures.

138 Well known as the cover picture for C.W. Hawkins' *The Story of Alton*, this is the blacksmith's shop at the rear of 14 Market Street after it had been taken over by Alfred Trimmer, seen here in this *c.*1900 view, holding the pipe. The brick and weatherboard shop opened out onto the cobbled Loe's Alley. In the background two of Mr. Loe's carts stand in front of the open doors of their sheds, which still exist.

139 The building on the left, currently the offices of the *Alton Herald*, was referred to as 'modern' in 1930. The four cottages were demolished in 1926 to make way for the new poultry market. In turn, that was replaced by Westbrook Walk in 1989. The building bearing the advertisement for 'Wright' in this *c*.1920 view is of medieval date and known at one time as 'Coppid Hall'. The home of 'Sooty' Wright, whose book *From Chimney Boy to Councillor* was published in 1931, provides a fascinating story of one man's life in Alton.

140 At the time of the 1666 map the *Black Boy* stood on this site, but it was rebuilt in the 18th century and around 1900 became the town's first cycle shop. Immediately to the right is the *Market Hotel*, formerly the *Butcher's Arms*, rebuilt *c*.1880. At the present time there is a wooden building on this site which was a former First World War army hut, later used for auctions of market produce.

141 The building in the previous picture had gone by the time this photograph was taken on 24 June 1919 and the vacant site was being used for the market. Livestock sales closed in 1966, although poultry continued for another ten years. The deadstock auctions came to an end in 1986. The 18th-century house known as Lady Place, in the corner of Market Square, was acquired as the site of a proposed new library. However, it was demolished and the site was incorporated into the car park.

142 Altonians turned out in large numbers on Monday 20 July 1908 to listen to General Booth, the grand old man of the Salvation Army. The 80-year-old stood in his open car in the Market Square and spoke for ten minutes to an appreciative crowd. The AUDC did not attend and were strongly rebuked for failing to honour such an important visitor!

143 No. 7 Cross & Pillory Lane, seen here *c.*1890, can be identified on the map of 1666 and was occupied by Moses Neave who had probably built it. The windows were altered *c.*1866 by Alexander Sayers and the adjoining house pulled down and alterations made 20 years later. The building on the left was used as a chapel and later became the Assembly Rooms until the new site opened at Crown Close in 1880. The site to the left was redeveloped as Cross and Pillory House which opened in 1983.

144 This view of Lenten Street *c.*1900 shows the house, on the right, which was built in 1702 by Nicholas Gates. Known as 'Brooklands', it was acquired by James Curtis *c.*1745. He had a tan yard at the bottom of the garden by the river. On 11 January 1746 a son, William, was born who in later years became famous as a botanist. In his honour the AUDC placed a commemorative plaque over the door and the house has since been named after him.

145 The Salvation Army came to Alton in 1883 and in September 1891 opened this building at the top of Amery Street. It survived until 1957, a year after this picture was taken, when it was demolished and more spacious premises built on the site. The new £16,000 building was opened by Lady Charlotte Bonham Carter of Wyck House, Binsted on 4 January 1958.

146 (*above*) In medieval times the area bounded by Cutpound Lane (now Amery Street) and Lenten Street had been associated with the cloth trade, at that time the most important industry in the town. All of the Amery Street properties seen here in 1936 had been proposed for demolition the previous year, but what is erroneously known as Spencer's House and the adjoining property were saved.

147 (*right*) The *Leathern Bottle* and the adjacent hop kilns, seen here *c*.1930, were associated with a brew house which had been on the site since at least the early 17th century. It was taken over by Moses Fielder in the early 19th century and subsequently acquired by J. & J. Knight, brewers of Farnham. After the *Leathern Bottle* closed in 1907 it became part of T. Lee & Sons, haulage contractors. Part of the site became an isolation hospital and the AUDC had offices and a yard there until 1931 when it was all cleared away and a new bus garage was built. It was in use until 1988, demolished two years later and redeveloped as offices which were first occupied in 1994.

148 (*above*) The large building on the left, on the corner of Butts Road and Tower Street, seen here *c*.1914, is the former police station built in 1845. Before then the police had occupied various premises in the town including Crown Hill and Normandy Street. After the existing police station in Orchard Lane was officially opened in December 1978, this site was cleared, and a new fire station was built which became operational in October 1981.

149 (*left*) This view of Butts Road *c*.1908 shows the entrance to the gas works on the left, an off licence, and the spire of All Saints' Church. Built by Messrs Dyers of Alton at a cost of some £3,500, the church was dedicated on 23 December 1874. A Sunday school and parish rooms were added in 1876 and in June the following year a day school was opened. All Saints' Infants' School closed in 1971 and the building is now Alton's Register Office.

FUNERAL PROCESSION.
Lt Col Mulvany, RAMC.
ALTON.
NOV 9th 05.

150 Although the funeral procession of the former Commanding Officer of the Princess Louise Hospital was a notable local event, this view also shows part of the gas works. The site, adjacent to Borovere Gardens, is currently occupied by a tyre depot. The building in the background is Sunnyside, a house built by George Frost in 1904, although it seems to have been altered since. Miss Bell's fountain is set in the gap between the two buildings.

151 The railway came to Alton with great celebrations on Monday 26 July 1852. When the line was extended to Winchester in 1865 the track was realigned to pass around the town and the present station was built. The original station, seen here on the left *c*.1905, was converted to the station master's house. It was subsequently demolished and the area is now part of the station car park.

152 The condition of the embankment associated with the railway bridge over Ashdell Road suggests that this view was taken shortly after the new line to Winchester was opened by the Mid Hants Railway on Monday 2 October 1865. The line was purchased by the London and South Western Railway in 1884 and became a secondary, although useful, diversionary route from Waterloo to Southampton.

153 Mr. Richardson, the station master, is seen here with his staff *c.*1880. A line to Basingstoke was opened on 1 June 1901 followed two years later by the Meon Valley line to Fareham. The former closed at the end of 1916 and the track was taken up and sent to France. It was not until 1924 that it re-opened, only to close for good 12 years later. The Fareham route closed in 1955 followed by the Winchester line in 1973, although this re-opened as a preserved railway between Alresford and Ropley four years later. The line was extended to Medstead in 1983 and the final link into Alton was made on 25 May 1985.

154 (*right*) The British School for Boys started in Church Street in 1843 and the following year moved to a room behind the Congregational church in Normandy Street. In 1845, due to increased numbers, this became the boys' school and the girls moved to Crowley's School room in Turk Street. In 1866 Frederick Crowley built and presented a new boys' school to the town, which was officially handed over on 1 May 1867. The girls' school moved to the same location 10 years later and the site is known today as Alton County Infants' School.

155 The school was built on the site of the house and forge of a blacksmith, and next door, Kearsley House, thought to have dated from 1600, was pulled down to make way for the girls' school. Development to the east beyond the town, seen on the 1666 map, was inevitable once the railway station had been built. The houses on the left date from *c*.1896, whilst on the right is the wall of Alton House which became a hotel in 1932, two years before this postcard was sent.

156 (*right*) The Cornish granite fountain, seen here at the Papermill Lane junction *c.*1925, was removed from Crown Close when the War Memorial was constructed in 1920. Following a road traffic accident it was removed by the AUDC, in 1964, and put in the public gardens some five years later, where it may still be seen today.

157 (*below*) This photograph of *c.*1910 is from the Littlefield Road junction looking towards the town. Up to *c.*1835 the land from Orchard Lane to Papermill Lane, and back almost as far as the river, was an open field which belonged to a West Worldham charity. By the time of the Tithe Commutation Award of 1839-41, Alton Lodge had been built for J.E. Spicer, who owned the papermill, and Alton House for the Rev. Bannister, curate of St Lawrence's Church.

158 (*below*) This view of Anstey Road *c.*1910, looking towards the town, shows a fine late Victorian terrace, now known as Wayvan Court, on the left. The railway lies behind the tree to the right of centre. The row of five cottages beyond was demolished and is now the site of the telephone exchange built in 1936.

159　A volunteer fire brigade was formed in 1863 and a Paxton manual engine was acquired but was replaced the following year by a Merryweather steam engine, the first one used outside London. The original engine house, seen here *c.*1885, was at the junction of Amery Street and Vicarage Hill.

160 The fire brigade, photographed here *c.*1910, moved to new premises in Cut Pound in 1891 next to what is now the back of the Community Centre. In 1922 they moved to the ground floor of the Town Hall and 12 years later moved again, this time to part of Westbrook House after it had been bought and adapted by the AUDC. The present building on Butts Road was occupied in October 1981.

161 Orps (or Haps) mill was close to Ashdell where the stream ran into King's Pond. It was one of a number of fulling mills along the river associated with the cloth trade. The cottages adjacent to the mill are seen here in this picture after a sketch of 1840 by Jane Curtis. The mill was demolished when the railway was extended some 25 years later.

162 Anstey mill enjoys a delightful rural location in this 1911 photograph. However, today the building looks rather different and is virtually hidden in the middle of Alton's industrial estate. Built of brick and local white sandstone, it was typical of most of the two hundred or so mills in the county which date from the 18th and 19th centuries.

163 The earliest paper makers in the town were William Barrett and later Robert Myears, although William King acquired the paper mill in 1775. He dammed the River Wey to form King's Pond as a reservoir for the mill machinery and was well known for his printing paper. In 1796 the mills were taken over by John Spicer, whose family continued to operate them until they closed in 1909. Some of the employees are seen here in 1877 in their characteristic folded paper caps.

164 Although the mill was disused during the First World War, the buildings were utilised to house German prisoners engaged on local agricultural work. In 1919 the Alton Battery Company took over the site and stayed for 40 years. Later occupants were Victoria Foundries and Beacon Packaging Services. The buildings, seen here in 1970, were badly damaged by fire in 1983 and the site was cleared for a housing development five years later.

165 The building business of Messrs J.H. & E. Dyer was one of the oldest in the town, having been started by John Dyer in 1784. The workforce, seen here c.1870, had an enviable record for church building and repair work including the rebuilding of Chawton church after the fire of March 1871.

166 Pearce's sawmills were founded in the 1890s by George Pearce, seen on the left in the long coat in this photograph of *c.*1905. The business, which was situated on Ackender Road and fronted onto Butts Road, produced a variety of domestic and commercial goods. Amongst these were wooden malt shovels, such as the one held by a workman in the middle row on the right.

167 During the Second World War the sawmills passed to the Alton Timber Co. Ltd. The site later ceased operating and the corner on Butts Road became Urquhart & Son's petrol station and car showroom which opened in 1955. It is currently the premises of Clover Leaf Cars. The photograph here was taken in 1958, before the remainder of the site on Ackender Road was also developed as a garage. Caffyns Ford now have a petrol station, showroom and workshops on the site.

168 (*above*) The Princess Louise Hospital, seen here in 1903, was the outcome of the 'Absent Minded Beggar' (AMB) relief fund, organised by the *Daily Mail* during the South African War of 1899-1902. It was opened by Princess Louise, Duchess of Argyle, in July 1903.

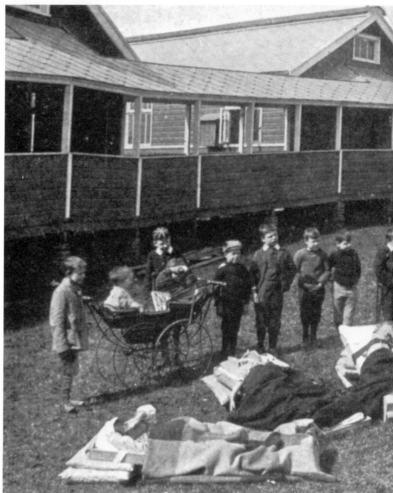

PRINCESS LOUISE HOSPITAL. ALTON. HANTS.

"Silverette"

169 (*above*) The appeal raised £35,000 which was matched by the *Daily Mail* and a 62-acre site was purchased from Mr. Montague Knight of Chawton House. The hospital, seen here *c*.1904, consisted of three blocks of 10 wards laid out in a fan shape, with all of the wards and central blocks connected by covered ways.

170 (*left*) The army hospital became surplus to requirements and in 1907 Sir William Treloar, who had taken a great interest in the care of crippled children when he was Lord Mayor of London, was granted the building to cure tuberculosis of the bones. At first the hospital and college facilities were side by side, but in the 1950s the Lord Mayor Treloar's College for Physically Handicapped Boys was opened at Froyle and the disabled girls were taught at the Florence Treloar's School at Holybourne. The schools have combined and the original hospital, which had been rebuilt in 1936, was an orthopaedic hospital until 1994. A community hospital, which opened in 1992, was built on part of the site. At the time of writing the future of the remainder of the site is still under discussion.

171 (*left*) Ackender Road, seen here *c*.1910, marked the boundary between the Langham Estate, to the right, and the remainder of the Whitedown Estate to the left. The former, sold in May 1903, was the property of Charles Kingsland and extended to what is now the public gardens. The latter belonged, in part, to the late George Gunner of Willhall Farm. It consisted of what is now King's Road, the upper part of Queen's Road and land fronting onto the Basingstoke Road, and was sold in June 1912.

172 (*below left*) Queen's Road, pictured here *c*.1920, was originally called All Saints' Road but only consisted of the buildings from the church on the corner to the terrace of Moss Rose Villas, built in 1878, and seen in no. 102. It seems that, following the Diamond Jubilee of Queen Victoria in 1897, the road was renamed. The plots for the houses seen here were sold by auction in October 1897 and by 1909 the road had been extended to Ackender Road, but it was not fully developed until after the Whitedown Estate sale of 1912.

173 (*below*) The Chauntsingers estate was purchased from the Hall family by the AUDC after the First World War. It was developed for housing in 1926-27 and access from Church Street involved the demolition of three cottages. The planted area on the right of this *c*.1927 picture was known as Warner's Folly after council member Stephen Warner. He was a local solicitor and Joint Honorary Curator at the Curtis Museum for some 20 years until his death in 1948.

174 (*right*) Nursery Cottages, seen here in 1936, were one of the few examples of 18th-century back-to-back dwellings in the town that survived into the 1930s. They were situated in what is now Nursery Road opposite the Boys' Club. The site was cleared and redeveloped for housing by AUDC in 1936-7.

175 (*below*) In 1947 the AUDC put up 35 temporary bungalows in Geales Crescent as a short-term solution to the urgent need for post-war housing. In the event, they lasted nearly four times as long as their designers intended, for the site was not redeveloped until 1985.

176 (*below*) Following suggestions by Councillor Warner, street names with local associations were chosen for the post-war council housing development at Anstey. This 1947 view shows building work in Dowden Grove. The Dowden family were land owners in the area in the 18th century and were associated with a private bank in Alton.

177 The Flood Meadows of today is a small part of the original meadow, seen here *c.*1920, much of which was developed for housing in the 1960s and '70s. The watercress beds were started by J. Mills around 1870, then carried on by his son, George, who lived in Tan House Lane until he retired in 1928. They were then taken over by Mr. Tabor, who had a business in the old Wey Iron Works, later converted into the Community Centre which opened in 1975.

178 Whitedown Lane has been an important route since at least the 18th century when there was a toll bar at the north end. Part of the road was realigned and improved in 1966. The following year the visibility at the Chawton Park Road cross-roads was also improved by the demolition of Miss Simmons' corner shop. The cottages on the left were renovated in the summer of 1972 and the thatch was replaced by tiles.

179 The New Odiham Road dates from 1839 when it formed a link from the *Golden Pot* to the Basingstoke turnpike near Willhall Farm. The toll cottage in the foreground dates from the same time and replaced one further along the Basingstoke Road. In 1936 a row of houses was built along the right side of the road. Thirty years later the toll cottage was demolished, and the junction improved, in advance of much of the Greenfields housing development. However, it was not until 1994 that a mini roundabout eased the traffic congestion.

180 With the toll house on the left and Willhall Farm on the right in this *c.*1900 view, the hillside in the middle distance provided the site of the Highridge housing development in the 1970s. With the Wootey and Greenfield housing areas off to the left of the picture, the fields beyond the town provided the space for the 1980s housing development of Borovere.

Bibliography

Bancroft P., *Railways around Alton—an illustrated bibliography* (1995)

Booth, A., *Alton in old picture postcards* (1994)

Curtis, W., *A Short History and Description of the Town of Alton* (1896)

Curtis, W.H., *The First Hundred Years of a Small Museum* (1955)

Friends of the Curtis Museum, *One Hundred Years on Crown Close* (1980)

Friends of the Curtis Museum, *Alton—Eastbrook Town Trail* (1980)

Hawkins, C.W., *The Story of Alton* (1973)

Hawkins, C.W., *And Still we Serve—a history of the Alton Volunteer Fire Brigade* (1988)

Hawkins, C.W. and Brice, M.H., *Alton—A Pictorial Biography* (1983)

Moynihan, G.S.E., *The Lord Mayor Treloar Hospital and College* (1988)

Victoria History of the Counties of England, Hampshire and the Isle of Wight, 5 volumes

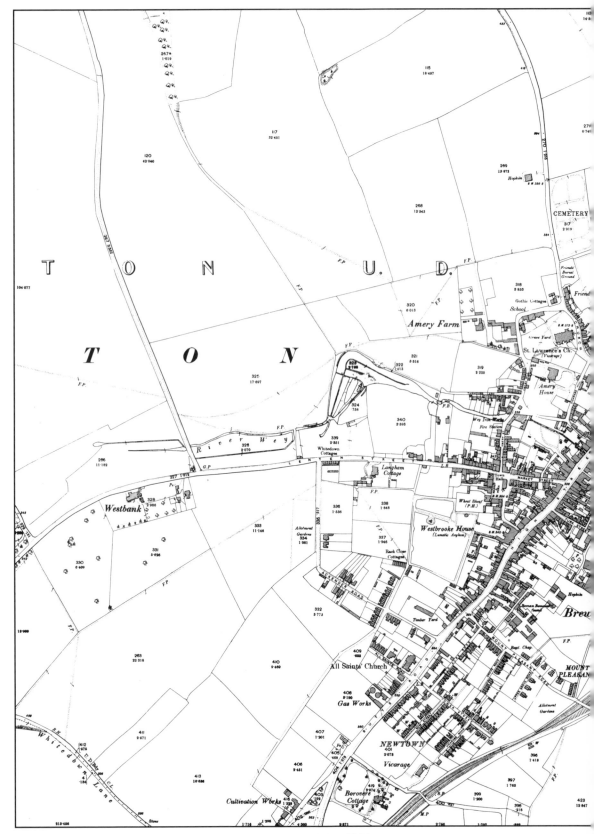

Ordnance Survey Map 1896.